Rookie
Read-About Science®

It Could Still Be a Desert WITHDRAWN

By Allan Fowler

Consultants

Linda Cornwell, Learning Resource Consultant,
Indiana Department of Education

Fay Robinson, Child Development Specialist

Lynne Kepler, Educational Consultant

ℚℙ Children's Press®
A Division of Grolier Publishing
New York   London   Hong Kong   Sydney
Danbury, Connecticut

Project Editor: Downing Publishing Services
Designer: Herman Adler Design Group
Photo Researcher: Caroline Anderson

Library of Congress Cataloging-in-Publication Data

Fowler, Allan.
    It could still be a desert / by Allan Fowler.
       p. cm. – (Rookie read-about science)
    Includes index.
    Summary: Describes the characteristics of deserts, the animals and
plants that live in them, and their constantly changing nature.
       ISBN 0-516-20319-3 (lib. bdg.)   0-516-26156-8 (pbk.)
       1. Deserts—Juvenile literature. [l. Deserts.] I. Title. II. Series
    GB612.F68   1997   98-28293
551.4'15–dc20   CIP
                                                                   AC

What sort of picture do you have in mind when you think about deserts? You might imagine a place like this one — sand, sand, and more sand, as far as you can see.

But not all deserts are covered by sand. Land could be covered by broken rocks and stones — and it could still be a desert.

It could be bare rock, with no soil or sand — and still be a desert.

A desert is any place that is very, very dry, and has little or no soil. It hardly ever rains in a desert.

Death Valley, in the western United States, is one of the world's driest and hottest places.

But a place could usually have mild or cool weather — and still be a desert.

Even deserts that are very hot during the day are likely to turn much cooler at night.

Only certain special kinds of plants and animals can live in a desert.

Cactus plants grow in deserts because they store water in their stems for a long time. Instead of leaves, they have sharp spines.

Cactuses come in many
shapes, and may grow
as big as a tree.

Some have colorful
flowers . . . or fruit you
can eat, like prickly pears.

Plants that need little water can grow in a desert.

Some desert plants bloom after a rainfall . . . live just a short time . . . and leave seeds to sprout and bloom after the next rain.

Other plants have long roots to reach water that is deep underground.

A place where camels, sheep, or goats graze could still be a desert.

Herdsmen wander with their flocks across deserts like the great Gobi Desert of China. These people, called nomads, live in tents called yurts.

Nomads of Arabia and North Africa dress in hooded cloaks, or burnooses.

A burnoose covers almost the entire body, yet fits loosely.

It helps protect the wearer against the hot desert sun and flying sand.

In Africa and Asia, camels or dromedaries carry people and their goods across deserts. That's why those animals are known

as "ships of the desert."
They can go several days
without water or food.
They store food, in the
form of fat, in their humps.

Dromedaries, or Arabian camels, have one hump. Bactrian camels, from central Asia, have two.

Snakes, lizards, mice, and birds are some of the animals you might find in a desert.

Also scorpions, which are related to spiders.

In a sandy desert, strong winds sometimes fill the air with swirling sand. People and animals must take cover during such a sandstorm.

The Sahara Desert, in Africa, is the world's largest desert.

Once it was grassland and
received plenty of rain.
But the weather became
drier, and, little by little,
the Sahara turned into
a sandy desert.

Now you can travel
hundreds of miles there
and not see a tree or a plant.

An oasis is a place in the desert where there is water. It may come from an underground spring. Date palms or other trees and plants grow in an oasis.

A desert could have farms,
and still be a desert. People
dig canals or lay pipelines
to bring water into a desert
from distant rivers or lakes.

Crops are now grown in such once-dry places as California's Imperial Valley and Israel's Negev Desert.

But most desert areas are too far from water for farming, or for many people to live there.

Life in a desert is hard.

How would you like to
live in a place where
people are grateful for
every drop of water?

Words You Know

Death Valley

Gobi Desert

Imperial Valley

Sahara Desert

30

bactrian camel

dromedary

burnoose

oasis

prickly pear

scorpion

snake

lizard

mouse

31

Index

About the Author

Allan Fowler is a free-lance writer with a background in advertising.
Born in New York, he lives in Chicago now and enjoys traveling.

Photo Credits

Cover: Beavertail cactus and monzonite